Cambridge Discovery

▶ INTERACTIVE I

Series editor: Bob Ha

A LIGHT IN THE NIGHT
THE MOON

Simon Beaver

CAMBRIDGE UNIVERSITY PRESS
Cambridge, New York, Melbourne, Madrid, Cape Town,
Singapore, São Paulo, Delhi, Mexico City

Cambridge University Press
32 Avenue of the Americas, New York, NY 10013-2473, USA

www.cambridge.org
Information on this title: www.cambridge.org/9781107647565

© Cambridge University Press 2014

This publication is in copyright. Subject to statutory exception and to the provisions of relevant collective licensing agreements, no reproduction of any part may take place without the written permission of Cambridge University Press.

First published 2014

Printed in Hong Kong, China, by Golden Cup Printing Company Limited

A catalog record for this publication is available from the British Library.

Library of Congress Cataloging-in-Publication Data

Beaver, Simon.
  A light in the night: the moon / Simon Beaver.
    pages cm. -- (Cambridge discovery interactive readers)
  ISBN 978-1-107-64756-5 (pbk. : alk. paper)
  1. Moon--Juvenile literature. 2. English language--Textbooks for foreign speakers. 3. Readers (Elementary) I. Title.

QB582.B43 2013
523.3--dc23

2013025125

ISBN 978-1-107-64756-5

Additional resources for this publication at www.cambridge.org

Cambridge University Press has no responsibility for the persistence or accuracy of URLs for external or third-party Internet Web sites referred to in this publication and does not guarantee that any content on such Web sites is, or will remain, accurate or appropriate.

Layout services, art direction, book design, and photo research: Q2ABillSMITH GROUP
Editorial services: Hyphen S.A.
Audio production: CityVox, New York
Video production: Q2ABillSMITH GROUP

Contents

Before You Read: Get Ready! 4

CHAPTER 1
The Man in the Moon 6

CHAPTER 2
A Helping Hand 8

CHAPTER 3
Lunatics 12

CHAPTER 4
Moon Stories 14

CHAPTER 5
What Do You Think? 20

After You Read 22

Answer Key 24

Glossary

Before You Read: Get Ready!

The Moon is very important in our lives. But how much do you know about it?

Words to Know

Look at the pictures. Then complete the sentences below with the correct words.

Earth   full moon   gods

rocket   space   telescope

1. There was a _____ last night. The sky was beautiful.
2. A _____ makes things bigger when you look at them.
3. The _____ is our home. It's where we live.
4. Thousands of years ago, the Romans had a lot of different _____.
5. You have to travel in a _____ to go into _____.

Words to Know

Read the text. Then complete the sentences below with the correct highlighted words.

Do you know about the tide? The Moon goes around the Earth and it pulls the sea. Every day, the sea comes up and covers the beach. In every season – winter, spring, fall, or summer – there are different tides. In England, there's a very old story about an important man called Cnut. He told the sea to stop. That was crazy! The tide *always* comes in and then goes out again.

1. He's a bad boy. He often _____ his sister's hair.
2. Are you _____? You can't go out in the snow with no shoes!
3. This book is about people who live on the Moon. It's a great _____.
4. The _____ is coming in. Don't leave your clothes near the water!
5. In Russia in winter, the snow _____ everything.
6. I like to go to Russia in summer. It's my favorite _____ there.
7. We went to the beach and swam in the _____.

The tide is going out.

CHAPTER 1

The Man in the Moon

HOW DID WE GET TO KNOW THE MOON?

Long ago, people in every part of the world looked up at the sky, the same way we do now. The two most important things they saw were the Sun and the Moon.

The Sun gave a lot of light, but the Moon gave only a little. So many people thought the Sun was a man god, and the Moon a woman god – a goddess.

And people saw a face on the Moon. They called it "the Man in the Moon." Parents still tell their children about him today.

Video Quest

Looking at the Moon

Watch the video. What did Galileo learn about the Moon with his telescope?

Then people studied **astronomy,** and they thought about how the Moon changed. In the end, the astronomers understood. The Moon was a big ball!

They understood that the Moon and the Earth go around the Sun. The Sun shines light on half of the Earth all the time – this gives us day and night. The Sun shines on half of the Moon all the time, too. But from Earth, we can't always see all of the light on the Moon. When the half of the Moon with light is away from us, the sky is dark. This is called a new moon. When we can see all of the light on the Moon, it's a full moon. Between the new moon and the full moon, there are half moons and crescent moons.

half moon

new moon

full moon

crescent moon

7

CHAPTER 2

A Helping Hand

HOW DOES THE MOON HELP THE EARTH?

In 1969, three American **astronauts** flew in a **rocket** to the Moon. Neil Armstrong was the first man to walk on the Moon. When he was there, he talked to people on Earth on the radio. But they heard him 1.25 **seconds** later. That's because it's more than 350,000 **kilometers** from the Moon to the Earth.

The Moon pulls the Earth. Because of this, the Earth is turning more and more slowly. Our day is getting 0.000015 seconds longer every year. But, of course, we don't feel the difference.

The Moon goes around the Earth, but really, the Earth and the Moon go around each other. At the same time, the Earth and the Moon, together, go around the Sun.

The Earth has a tilt of 23.5 degrees. Because of the pull of the Moon, this tilt doesn't change. And that's a good thing, because it's the Earth's tilt that gives us our seasons. Thanks to the Moon, we enjoy spring, summer, fall, and winter. And the Earth doesn't get too hot or too cold for life.

The Moon keeps the Earth's tilt the same.

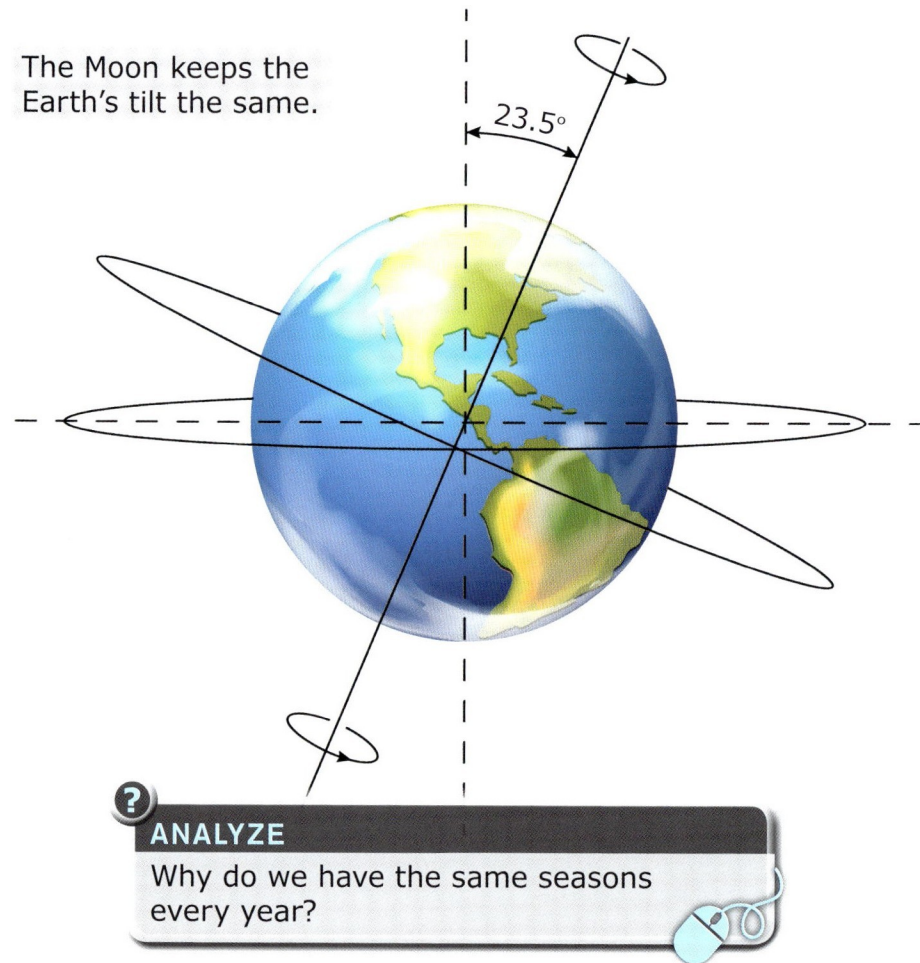

ANALYZE
Why do we have the same seasons every year?

High tide   Low tide

The Moon's pull gives us tides, too. The Moon pulls the sea, and the water goes up and down. The Sun also pulls the sea and gives us tides, but the Moon's tides are much bigger because it is closer to the Earth.

Tides can help us. We can use them to make **electricity** for our factories and homes. And that electricity is clean to make. It isn't bad for plants and animals.

The Moon also helps sailors on boats at sea. At night, they can see where the Moon is – if there are no clouds. Then they know where to go.

Video Quest

Moonlight

Watch the video. How does the Moon help baby turtles?

The Moon helps animals, too. Many animals go out at night. A little moonlight helps them to see.

Of course, for some small animals, that's not always a good thing. Big animals can see them in the moonlight and eat them!

The Moon can also tell animals where to go. Baby olive ridley turtles start their life in a hole in the sand on a beach. They use the Moon to find the sea.

A hole in the sand

A baby olive ridley turtle

11

Aristotle

CHAPTER 3

Lunatics

CAN THE MOON MAKE PEOPLE CRAZY?

The word *lunar* is the adjective we use for the Moon. It comes from Latin, the language of the Ancient[1] Romans. They called the Moon "Luna." And *lunatic* is an old English word for a crazy person. A long time ago, people thought the Moon changed people. Lunatics went crazy when the Moon was full.

The Ancient Greek thinker and teacher Aristotle said this was because there was too much light from the full moon. Some people couldn't sleep. That made them crazy.

[1] **ancient:** from a very long time ago

Was he right? We now have streetlights to see at night. People don't go crazy because of streetlights. But we know that people in countries with no night in the summer or no sunlight in the winter can have problems. We need both day and night.

Today, it's often bad to use the word "lunatic." England stopped using the word in its laws[2] in 1930. But people still use it when they talk. For example, if someone is a crazy driver, we say, "He drives like a lunatic!"

[2] **laws:** what people in a country must and mustn't do

? UNDERSTAND
Why did Aristotle think the Moon made people crazy?

Streetlights

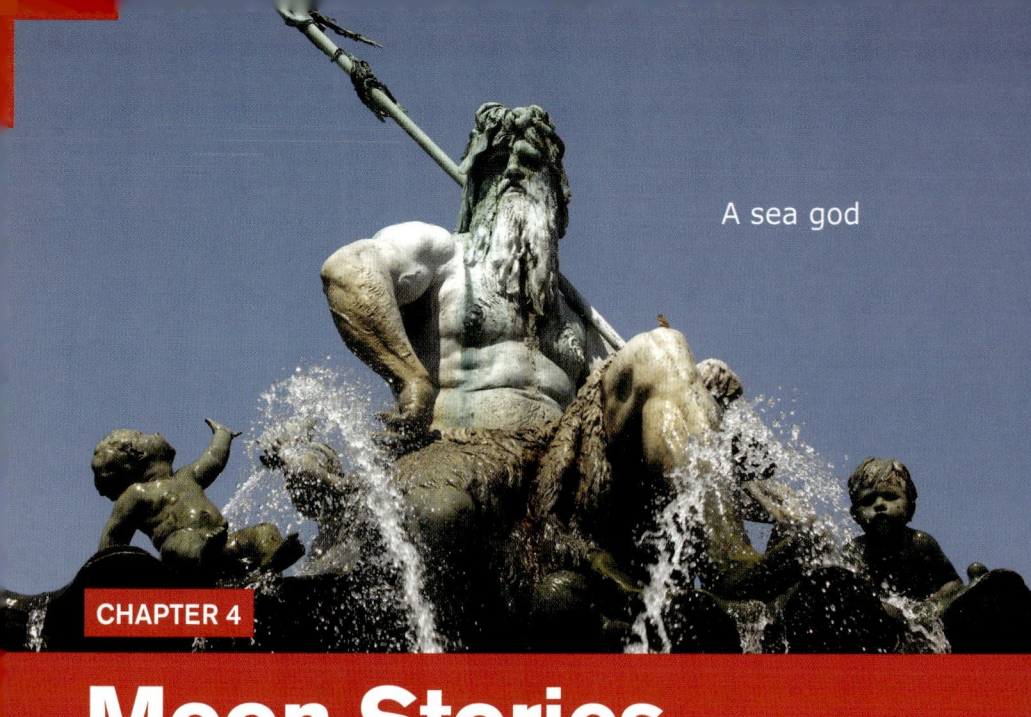

A sea god

CHAPTER 4

Moon Stories

WHY IS THE MOON SO INTERESTING?

There are old stories about the Moon in every country.

The Maoris were the first people in New Zealand. They lived there before Europeans came. One old Maori story is about Rona. Rona was the daughter of the sea god, Tangaroa. She made the sea go up and down at high and low tide.

One night, Rona had water in a bucket to take to her children at home. She could see where to go in the moonlight. But then a cloud in the sky covered the Moon.

Rona couldn't see. She said some bad things about the Moon. But the Moon heard her and was very **angry**. It pulled Rona up into the sky!

Today, many Maoris see a woman and a bucket in the Moon. They say that rain is water from Rona's bucket.

In another Maori story, a man – also called Rona – went to the Moon to find a wife. Every four weeks, the man eats his wife and then she eats him. That's why the dark and light parts of the Moon get bigger and smaller each month.

A bucket

An alien

A scientist

There are many stories about the Moon in science fiction books and movies. Science fiction is about what things are going to be like in a hundred, a thousand, or a million years. Or about worlds that are different from ours.

In 1901, H.G. Wells wrote a book called *The First Men in the Moon*. In the book, two men fly a rocket to the moon. They find different kinds of aliens there. Some aliens want to stop them leaving. In the end, one man goes home, but the other stays. Today, we know there's no life on the Moon. But in 1901, people didn't know that. Anything was possible.

In 1867, the USA wanted to buy Alaska from Russia. So they sent a scientist called George Davidson to study it. He wrote down what he saw, and the USA paid the Russians $7.2 million for Alaska.

Davidson, an astronomer, wanted to see an eclipse. So in 1869, he went back to Alaska, to a place called Chilkat Valley. Davidson told the people there, "The Sun's going to go dark tomorrow!" The Chilkats laughed. That was impossible, they thought. But the next day, the Moon went in front of the Sun. Everything was dark! Some Chilkats thought Davidson did it!

Video Quest

Eclipses

Watch the video. What are partial and total solar eclipses?

An eclipse

A werewolf

Silver

The Moon can change how we feel, but can it change us into animals?

In many countries, there are stories about people who change into birds, cats, or fish. Or werewolves! In the stories, people change into werewolves when the Moon is full. Some people change because a werewolf bites[3] them. They get big teeth and hair on all their body. Then they eat animals – or sometimes people!

Some stories say you can only kill[4] werewolves with silver, possibly because the color of the Moon is silver. The stories aren't true, but they make great movies!

[3] **bite:** People and animals use their teeth to bite.
[4] **kill:** end somebody's life

In an Ancient Greek story, a man called Lycaon doesn't think Zeus is really a god. To find out, Lycaon kills Zeus's son and cooks him for Zeus! But Zeus knows the food isn't animal meat. He's angry and changes Lycaon into a wolf. This is one of the oldest werewolf stories.

One of the newest is in the Harry Potter books. Harry's teacher, Remus Lupin, is a werewolf. Werewolves in stories are usually bad, but Lupin is a good man. So he isn't happy about being a werewolf.

ANALYZE
Why do people like stories about werewolves? Do you like them? What other werewolf stories do you know?

Zeus was an important god in Ancient Greek stories.

CHAPTER 5

What Do You Think?

TAKE A QUIZ ABOUT THE MOON. HAVE FUN!

Now you know some things about the moon. Here's a quiz with more information about it. Choose an answer. If you don't know, guess.

1. What ball is on the Moon?
   - Ⓐ a football
   - Ⓑ a golf ball
   - Ⓒ a basketball

2. What do some people say the Moon is made of?
   - Ⓐ green cheese
   - Ⓑ banana pizza
   - Ⓒ orange ice cream

3 Is there a dark **side** of the Moon?
- Ⓐ yes
- Ⓑ no
- Ⓒ Both sides are dark.

4 What is a "blue moon"?
- Ⓐ the second full moon in one month
- Ⓑ the second new moon in one month
- Ⓒ the second eclipse in one month

5 How hot does it get on the Moon?
- Ⓐ -20° C
- Ⓑ 25° C
- Ⓒ 125° C

6 Which came first?
- Ⓐ the Earth
- Ⓑ the Moon
- Ⓒ They're the same age.

....

Answers
1. B. In 1971, astronaut Alan Shepard hit a golf ball nearly half a kilometer on the Moon! It's still there.
2. A. In a story, someone saw the Moon in a river and thought it was cheese. So people said, "The Moon is made of green cheese."
3. B. We only see one side of the Moon from Earth, but the other side isn't dark all the time.
4. A. People say "once in a blue moon" to mean "almost never" because there aren't often two full moons in one calender month.
5. C. The days are very hot on the Moon. But at night, it can be -150° C. Take a warm coat!
6. C. Both are about 4,500,000,000 years old.

After You Read

True or False?

Choose Ⓐ (True) or Ⓑ (False). If the book does not tell you, choose Ⓒ (Doesn't say).

1 Neil Armstrong talked to his wife from the Moon on the radio.
   - Ⓐ True
   - Ⓑ False
   - Ⓒ Doesn't say

2 It's a good thing that the tilt of the Earth doesn't change.
   - Ⓐ True
   - Ⓑ False
   - Ⓒ Doesn't say

3 Tides are bigger in the spring and fall.
   - Ⓐ True
   - Ⓑ False
   - Ⓒ Doesn't say

4 Baby olive ridley turtles start their life in the sea.
   - Ⓐ True
   - Ⓑ False
   - Ⓒ Doesn't say

5 The word *lunar* is the adjective we use for the Sun.
   - Ⓐ True
   - Ⓑ False
   - Ⓒ Doesn't say

6 Maoris think that Rona was the daughter of a sea god.
   - Ⓐ True
   - Ⓑ False
   - Ⓒ Doesn't say

7 The two men in H.G. Wells's book meet aliens.
- (A) True
- (B) False
- (C) Doesn't say

8 In stories, people change into werewolves at the new moon.
- (A) True
- (B) False
- (C) Doesn't say

Complete the Text

Use the words in the box to complete the paragraph.

astronaut	kilometers	rocket	space

Neil Armstrong was an American **1** _____. He went into **2** _____. He went to the Moon on a **3** _____. He was the first person to walk on the Moon. He traveled more than 700,000 **4** _____ to the Moon and back.

Lunar Stories

Think of three stories where the Moon is important. What kind of story is it (book, movie, TV show, comic book)? Why is the Moon important?

Name of story	Kind of story	Why is the Moon important?

Answer Key

Words to Know, page 4
❶ full moon ❷ telescope ❸ Earth ❹ gods
❺ rocket, space

Words to Know, page 5
❶ pulls ❷ crazy ❸ story ❹ tide ❺ covers
❻ season ❼ sea

Video Quest, page 7
Galileo learned that the light and dark parts of the Moon were really the high and low parts.

Analyze, page 9
We have the same seasons because the Earth's tilt doesn't change. It doesn't change because of the pull of the Moon.

Video Quest, page 11
The baby turtles see the Moon and go to it.

Understand, page 13
The light stopped people from sleeping.

Video Quest, page 17
partial: the Moon only covers part of the Sun
total: the Moon covers all of the Sun

Analyze, page 19 *Answers will vary.*

True or False?, page 22
❶ C ❷ A ❸ C ❹ B ❺ B ❻ A ❼ A ❽ B

Complete the Text, page 23
❶ astronaut ❷ space ❸ rocket ❹ kilometers

Lunar Stories, page 23 *Answers will vary.*